I am a Reform Jew

A Workbook Diary for EXPLAINING REFORM JUDAISM

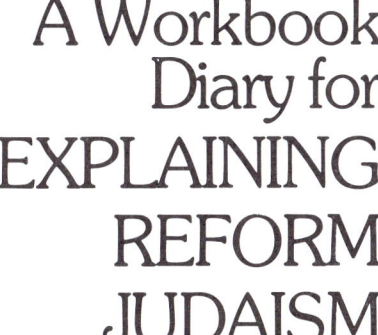

by Kerry Olitzky and Naomi Patz

BEHRMAN HOUSE, INC. · PUBLISHERS · SPRINGFIELD, NEW JERSEY

For Avi and Jesse,
our future in Reform Judaism.
K.O.

For Masha, Yisrael, and Naomi, in Leningrad; and for Matthew, Elizavetta, Lev, and Anna, in Moscow: *l'shanah ha-ba'ah b'yerushalayim!*
N.P.

Book design by Gene Siegel

11 Edison Place, Springfield, NJ 07081
www.behrmanhouse.com

5
ISBN 0-87441-448-2

Manufactured in the United States of America

Contents

To the Student

The book you are holding is both a workbook and a diary of your experiences as you learn about Reform Judaism. When you have completed the course, keep this book as a record. Over the years you will want to refer to it again to see how you and your ideas have changed and grown.

After working with *Explaining Reform Judaism* and this workbook, we hope that you will know with great certainty what you mean and why you are proud when you say "I am a Reform Jew."

About the Photographs

Without worship and study, there would be no Judaism. But synagogue and religious school are not the whole story. Wherever Jews get together in a Jewish setting, Judaism is there, too. Throughout this book are pictures of young people working and playing together in Jewish settings such as synagogue youth groups, summer camps, weekend retreats, community centers, and volunteer programs.

We have included these photographs to introduce you to the world of activities available to young Reform Jews. Each photograph shows yet another way of saying: "I am a Reform Jew." Each photograph shows another way for you to find your own place in Reform Judaism.

We would like to thank the following people and organizations for the photographs:

NFTY (North American Federation of Temple Youth). NFTY is the national organization of all the regional youth groups in the country, which are in turn made up of the youth groups of individual synagogues.

Pages 36 and 56 (courtesy of Naomi Patz); page 75 (courtesy of the New Jersey-West Hudson Valley Council of the Union of American Hebrew Congregations).

Kutz Camp Institute, in Warwick, New York. Kutz is the national camp of NFTY. The participants are people of high school age who come to Kutz for a summer of friendship, recreation, and Jewish learning. During the school year, youth groups converge on Kutz Camp for weekend retreats.

Pages 13, 17, 20 (photo by Steve Goodman), 26, 31, 33, 58, 61, 71, 78, 81 and 85.

Eisner Camp, in Great Barrington, Massachusetts. Under the direction of the Union of American Hebrew Congregations Youth Division, Eisner is a summer camp for participants aged 8–16.

Pages 28 and 42.

JFTY Urban Mitzvah Corps. A summer program for high school students run by the New Jersey Federation of Temple Youth. The participants volunteer in community services, helping out in a nursing home, a day camp for the handicapped children, two inner city playgrounds, a day camp for underprivileged children, and a soup kitchen for the homeless. The volunteers live together in a communal house on the campus of Rutgers University in New Brunswick, New Jersey.

Pages 48 and 64 (photos by Robert L. Kern).

The JWB in New York City. The JWB is the central national organization for all the Y's and Jewish Community Centers in the country. These centers are places where Jews of all ages and from all the different movements can get together for such programs as holiday celebrations, cultural programs, classes, and sports activities. They also sponsor summer camps and day camps.

Pages 2 and 10.

Getting Started

WHO AM I?

Fill in this survey about yourself, your family, your school and your synagogue. Ask your parents and teachers for help if you need it.

Your name ______________________________

Your Hebrew name ______________________________

Your age ______________________________

The name of your school ______________________________

The name of your synagogue ______________________________

The name of your teacher ______________________________

Do you call yourself a Reform Jew? ______

Describe Reform Judaism in one sentence: ______________________________

____

When did your first ancestors come to America? ______________________________

In what country(ies) had they lived before? ______________________________

Were they Reform Jews? ______ If they weren't, what was their religious affiliation? ______________

Where did they first live when they came to this country? ______________________________
(city/state)

What did your great grandparents do for a living? ______________________________

What about your grandparents? ______________________________

What are your parents' occupations? ______________________________

Who was the first person in your family to go to college? ______________________________

When did your family move to the community you live in now? ______________________________

What synagogues have you belonged to (either in this community or in the old ones)? ___________

____

Were they Reform congregations?_____ If not, with what movement in Judaism were they affiliated?

____

How long ago did the first member of your family (parents, grandparents, great-grandparents) join this congregation? ____

Do any of your other relatives belong to Reform congregations? ___________________

If not, what is their religious affiliation? ___________________________________

In what year was your synagogue founded? ____________________________________

Is it officially connected to the Reform movement? ______________________________

At a Jewish day camp near Hartford, Connecticut, a counselor and campers recite the blessings over Sabbath candles and hallah. By teaching children how to perform the *mitzvot* of *Kabbalat Shabbat*—welcoming the Sabbath—the counselor is also performing another valuable *mitzvah*—educating others. There are many different ways of "doing mitzvot."

DIARY:
DOING MITZVOT

Think about what you've done today. Using this page, record all of your actions—everything you can remember having done. Write each one here.

Examples:

I woke up for school at 6:30 a.m.
I brushed my teeth and washed my face.
I helped my brother get dressed.
I gave my homework to my teachers.

Judaism says that *mitzvot* are the things that God demands from each of us as loving, caring beings. How many of what you have listed would you consider *mitzvot*? (In the examples above, the first would be "taking responsibility," the second "respect for my body," the third "helping others, love, respect for parents" and the fourth, "study, respect for teachers.") See how many *mitzvot* you can identify in your own list, and write them next to each entry.

PHOTO ALBUM

This workbook is illustrated with photographs of young people working and playing together in Jewish settings, such as synagogues, summer camps, weekend retreats, community centers, and volunteer programs. Take a moment to go through the book and look at the photographs.

Use this page to preserve some photographs of your own. Attach one picture of yourself, than add whatever others you like: you and your family, you and your friends, you involved in a favorite activity. Try to include a Jewish activity, such as building a sukkah, lighting Hanukkah candles, putting on a Purim play, or participating in a Bar or Bat Mitzvah. Then write a caption explaining each photo.

1: A New Movement Modernizes Judaism

*IDENTIFIERS**

In Chapter One, the authors tell you about places in Europe where Jews had to wear special identification. List three examples:

____

____

______________________________________.

Why were they forced to wear them? ______________________________________

____

We live in a land of freedom, where people *choose* to show their identification with a religious or ethnic group. In the space below, create a bumper sticker that you would be proud to put on your automobile, or on your notebook or on your locker to show that you are a Jew.

*Answers to all starred exercises are in the Answer Key at the end of the book.

Do you think people wear *kippot* or six-pointed stars for that reason—to show others that they are special, that they are Jews? ______

Do you ever wear such an identifying symbol? ______

If you do, what do you wear? ______

Why is this an important symbol? What special meaning does it have for you? ______

______

If you choose not to wear an "identifier," is it for any particular reason? ______

______

GETTING THE PICTURE

Study the photograph on page 3 of the textbook. Compare it to your own street. In what ways that you can *see* does the Frankfurt ghetto appear different from your neighborhood?

______

______

______

In what ways that you can *imagine*? (For example, how many families do you think lived in those buildings?)

______

______

______

______

______

______

______

______

______

SCRAMBLED WORDS*

These scrambled words hold the key to yet another word. Rearrange the letters to find the answers to each of the clues below.

1. BONSACJO — Israel ______________, the "father of Reform Judaism."

   _ _ _ _ _ _ (_) _

2. NEESES — This town was the site of the first Jewish school where boys and girls studied together.

   (_) _ _ _ _ _

3. MENTAINOCAPI — The process by which Jews became citizens.

   (_) _ _ _ _ _ _ _ _ _ _ _

4. TEGOHT — Name of the walled neighborhoods where Jews were forced to live.

   _ _ _ _ _ _

5. UNOOVILERT — The French ______________ began in 1789.

   (_) _ _ _ _ _ _ _ _ _

6. CENARF — The first European country to give Jews the rights of citizenship.

   (_) _ _ _ _ _

7. NAGREMY — The country where Reform Judaism began.

   _ _ (_) _ _ _ _

Now unscramble the circled letters to find the name of an important development in Judaism.

_____ _____ _____ _____ _____ _____

THE FRENCH REVOLUTION*

The beginning of this chapter is about the French Revolution. What was the revolution about? ______

____

What new freedoms did French Jews gain as a result of the French Revolution? ______

____

How did this help Jews in other parts of the world? ______

____

WHICH DON'T BELONG?*

The following questions refer to Jewish life in Europe just before the Emancipation. Circle the examples that do not belong in each group.

1. Permitted Jewish occupations:

law

money lending

selling second-hand clothing

dentistry

junk dealing

2. Organization of Jewish community life:

speaking a special Jewish language

settling disputes in Jewish law courts

living by the Jewish calendar

sending young Jews to be educated in Christian schools

3. Reform innovations:

"mixed" choir

church services

Christians and Jews worshipping together

shorter services

services in the local language

*MORE OR LESS**

Israel Jacobson, considered by some to be the "father" of Reform Judaism, made many changes in worship services. Did he

1. make services *more* or *less* formal?__________

2. include *more* or *less* Hebrew?__________

3. give women *more* or *less* participation?__________

4. include *more* or *less* Western influence?__________

List some of the other reforms he introduced into services. ____________________________

____

What do you think was Jacobson's most important contribution to Reform Judaism? ____________

____

Many people can draw, some better than others, but no two people draw in exactly the same way. In developing her own special talent for creative expression, this young artist shows one example of what is meant by "being special."

DIARY: BEING SPECIAL

The name of the first part of your textbook is "What Makes Reform Jews Special?" Without consulting a dictionary, write down your idea of the meaning of the word special. List some of the things that make you special.

Examples:

I twinned with a refusenik at my Bar/Bat Mitzvah.
I play the violin.
I'm on the soccer team.

Now, go back and place a star next to those things that you think are special because you are Jewish.

Example:

I say the shema *before I go to bed.*

Being special involves a relationship to someone or something. One thing that is special about each of us is that we are, in a way, each at the center of our own world. Part of that specialness is how we relate to other people and to the various aspects of our lives.

Make a drawing of yourself at right and, using the answers you wrote above, draw something that represents each aspect of your specialness. Draw a line from you to each thing or person, and copy what you wrote on the line.

Can everything that is special about you be expressed in a drawing—or even in words? Some parts of being special have to do with the way we feel—about ourselves and about other people. Sometimes these can be expressed through our actions; sometimes, they are deep inside, waiting for the right time.

2: A Revolutionary Idea

*TRUE OR FALSE**

Write T (for True) or F (for False) next to each sentence.

1. Leopold Zunz was the first Reform Jew. ________
2. The leaders of the Jewish community were enthusiastic about the innovations made by the Reformers. ________
3. The community leadership offered the Reformers a chance to hold services in the chapel of the largest synagogue in Berlin. ________
4. The community leadership complained to the Prussian authorities about what the Reformers were doing. ________
5. Leopold Zunz majored in Jewish Studies at university. ________
6. Leopold Zunz used the techniques of modern scholarship to study Jewish subjects. ________
7. *Wissenschaft des Judentums* helps cure upset stomachs. ________
8. Leopold Zunz proved that the preaching of sermons had been part of Judaism for many centuries. ________

MIDRASH

Read the *midrash* on page 14 in the textbook and explain it below. What does it tell us about the way Torah (and Judaism) has changed and developed?

____

____

____

____

A quiet Shabbat afternoon at Kutz Camp.

*WHAT AND HOW**

As the textbook tells you, in 1823 the King of Prussia issued orders that limited the new freedoms of the French Revolution and the reforms that were being instituted by Leopold Zunz and other Jews in the community. What orders did the King of Prussia give?

____

How did the new restrictions affect the Reformers? ______________________

____

*PROVING HIS POINT**

Leopold Zunz used the "scientific method" of studying Judaism. To prove his point about sermons, he studied______________. Its chief purpose seems to be the teaching of______________ in ways that offer people______________________.

Zunz was convinced that these books were really collections of ______________________.

*UNSCRAMBLE THIS**

CONFUSING, WHEN MANY LEOPOLD OF DEVELOPMENT HISTORICAL UNSCRAMBLE ZUNZ OF INFORMATION LEARN WANTED SERMONS PIECES ABOUT THE HAD HE TO TO.

IMAGINARY DIARY: LEAVING THE GHETTO

Imagine that you and your family are Jews living in nineteenth-century Europe. Something incredible has happened—the Emancipation! Now you can leave the ghetto and move to a new house in a nice neighborhood. You want to go to a school where you can study math and science and secular history. You want to be able to get a good job. Write an imaginary diary entry, describing your conversation with your parents when you tell them of your plans to leave the ghetto. What would be your arguments for leaving? (What does the textbook say?) What would your parents' objections be?

3: Reform Comes to America

WAVES OF IMMIGRATION*

America is a land of immigrants. We often forget this fact because some of our families have been here for a number of generations. Our ancestors didn't all come here at the same time, however. The first Jewish immigrants came to America in the________________century from________________-and________________-speaking countries. Later, there were two great waves of Jewish immigration. The first, in the________________s, brought Jews from________________, primarily________________. In the second, which began in________________and lasted until________________, thousands upon thousands of Jews from________________came to the United States.

IDEALS OF AN ERA*

An excerpt from the *Union Prayer Book* of 1895 is reprinted on page 26 of the text. In the left column below are some phrases taken from that prayer. Can you match these phrases with the Jewish ideals that they express? Place the letter of an ideal in the right column next to each of the phrases in the left column.

______	1. "we of the household of Israel"	A. one God for all people
______	2. "we think of all men as Thy children"	B. Jews are all members of one large family
______	3. "our common Father"	C. all people should be treated fairly
______	4. "we grow sensitive to the indignities and injustices visited upon our fellow men"	D. all people are created equal

*A FILL-IN ON MESSIANISM**

Fill in the blanks with words from the box above them. Be careful—there are more words than you need.

JERUSALEM	**ZOMBIES**	**PURIFIED**	**GRAVES**	**HEAVEN**	**SOULS**

Traditional Judaism believes that when the Messiah comes, all the ________ will open, people's ________ will return to their ________ bodies, and everyone will appear before God in ________ for the Day of Judgment.

CONSCIENCE	**DIES**	**GRANDPARENT**	**SOULS**	**SPARK**	**MUSAF**

Reform Judaism rejected these beliefs but still had questions: What puts the ________ of life into matter? What makes humans the only animals with a ________? Why do human beings have ________? And what happens to the soul when a person ________?

WORDS FOR WISE

Rabbi Isaac M. Wise, the great organizer of Reform Judaism in America, did not have an easy career. When he was serving a congregation in Albany, New York, he got into trouble because of his beliefs. Imagine that you can see into that congregation's synagogue on Rosh Hashanah in 1850. Either draw a cartoon that shows what happened or recreate your version of the argument between Rabbi Wise and the president of the congregation on the subject of belief in the Messiah.

DIARY: A PRAYER FOR PEACE

Write your own prayer for peace, using the examples on pages 27-28 of the textbook as a guide.

4: Reform Jews and Other Jews in Our Day

LOOKING AT PICTURES

Look at the ritual objects in the photographs on pages 30-34. Chose two ritual objects and compare them.

I have chosen the ____________________ on page _______ and the ____________________ on page_______.

Is the first old or new?____________________ I can tell because ______________________________.

Is the second one old or new?____________________ I can tell because __________________________.

The first was made in (name of country, if given)____.

The second was made in (name of country, if given) _______________________________________.

The name of the person who crafted the first ritual object is ______________________________.

The name of the person who crafted the second ritual object is_____________________________.

The first ritual object is used ____.

The second ritual object is used ____.

I like the____________________ritual object better than the____________________because __________

____.

These photographs are in the textbook to demonstrate that__________________________________

____.

LOOK AND SAY

Although most Reform Jews do not use the *mikveh*, some Reform rabbis require its use for conversion. There is a picture of a *mikveh* on page 36 of the textbook. Look at the illustration carefully and describe what you think is happening.

____

____

____

IF YOU MADE THE REQUIREMENTS

Imagine that you have been asked to speak to someone who is interested in converting to Judaism. What reasons might that person give for wanting to become Jewish?

____

____

Pages 34-37 of the text talk about the Reform and more traditional requirements for conversion and the problems that can arise. With these in mind, what would *you* require in order for someone to be officially converted to Judaism?

____

____

____

How would you describe your requirements? (check one)

______ easy to fulfill

______ hard to fulfill

Why do you think it should be easy/hard to convert to Judaism? ______________________

____

____

Do you think that your requirements would satisfy the Orthodox or Conservative movements? Why or why not?

____

CHOOSING

Here are a few questions about freedom of choice:

1. Do you believe that Jews should be able to make up their own minds about all areas of ritual observance?______
2. Can someone not believe in God and still be a Jew?______
3. Is every Jew who doesn't keep kosher necessarily a Reform Jew?______
4. Are there any areas of Jewish life or belief about which you think there should be no choice?______

   If you have answered yes, what are they? ____

   ____

Relaxing after activities at the JFTY (New Jersey Federation of Temple Youth) week-long summer conclave.

*A SAMPLE TEST**

Often we expect more of people who choose to become Jews than we do of people who are born Jewish. Here is part of a short review test that a Reform rabbi may require of converts, or Jews-by-choice. Can you pass it? List the ten holidays named here in their correct chronological order, starting from Rosh Hashanah. (Careful—not every term listed is a holiday.)

SIDDUR
ARON HAKODESH
TORAH
PESAH
KADDISH
TISHA B'AV
BIMAH
SHAVUOT
ROSH HASHANAH
NER TAMID
ALIYAH
MINYAN
TU B'SHEVAT

SUKKOT
PURIM
SIMHAT TORAH
BAR MITZVAH
BAT MITZVAH
YOM KIPPUR
HAFTARAH
HANUKKAH
AMIDAH
SHEMA

1. Rosh Hashanah
2. ______________
3. ______________
4. ______________
5. ______________
6. ______________
7. ______________
8. ______________
9. ______________
10. ______________

REFORM RABBIS IN ISRAEL

All rabbis are considered to be "rabbis in Israel," that is, religious leaders of the Jewish people. However, only a few people have actually been ordained as Reform rabbis in the State of Israel. On page 37 of the textbook is a picture of Rabbi Alfred Gottschalk ordaining Mordecai Rotem. Why do the authors call this moment historic?

____

____

____

DIARY: A SYNAGOGUE VISIT

Do you have friends who belong to other synagogues in your community? Go with them to services one day. Then make a comparison between the services of their synagogue and those of your own.

Start by writing the name of the synagogue, the movement it belongs to, and the date of your visit.

Things to look for:

What prayer book does the congregation use?
Do men and women sit together?
How long are the services?
How many of the prayers are said in Hebrew, in English, or both?
What melodies are used?
Does anyone wear a kippah *and/or* tallit*? Who?*

(Do not bring a pen and paper. Orthodox Jews and many Conservative Jews don't write on Shabbat, and it is not appropriate to write during services. Remember your impressions and write them down later.)

5: What All Jews Share

FAMILY CELEBRATIONS

How does the textbook distinguish between "tradition" and "traditions"?

The tradition is____.

Traditions are____.

Some special family traditions get passed from one generation to another. Some are developed together (like who sits in which seat at the table, what you do on birthdays or on Hanukkah and Thanksgiving or on the day you come home from camp). Invent a new tradition for your family. Write it here.

What is the purpose of this tradition, and what, if anything, does it replace?

Do you think that your family would actually accept your "tradition"? Can traditions be imposed or must they develop naturally?

PLURALISM

The word pluralism describes the approach Reform Jews take to Jewish religious practices. It suggests that there is enough room in Judaism for people to have different approaches toward belief and observance. After reading the chapter, write down why you think pluralism is so important to Reform Judaism.

*BAR AND BAT MITZVAH**

Based on the description of a Bar/Bat Mitzvah on page 43, what do you think is the most important aspect of the ceremony, one that is shared by all Jews?

____

____

DIFFERENCES WITHIN UNITY

Find and circle the hidden words.

ASHKENAZI BRIT MILAH CONSERVATIVE CONVERT GOOD DEEDS HASIDIC HOLOCAUST ISRAEL JEWS ORTHODOX REFORM JUDAISM REFUSENIK SEPHARDI TZEDAKAH UNITY

X	G	K	I	N	E	S	U	F	E	R
G	O	O	D	D	E	E	D	S	V	E
B	R	I	T	M	I	L	A	H	I	F
H	Z	Q	C	O	N	V	E	R	T	O
O	A	L	L	S	H	A	R	E	A	R
L	S	E	P	H	A	R	D	I	V	M
O	H	A	S	I	D	I	C	M	R	J
C	K	R	J	K	L	M	N	O	E	U
A	E	S	T	E	N	O	P	F	S	D
U	N	I	T	Y	W	X	O	Y	N	A
S	A	I	J	K	L	S	T	U	O	I
T	Z	E	D	A	K	A	H	H	C	S
M	I	O	R	T	H	O	D	O	X	M

COMMON TO ALL*

This sentence has one beginning and many possible endings. Put a T (for True) next to the conclusions you think are correct, and an F (for False) next to the statements you know are wrong.

Every movement in Judaism believes that it is right to

1. observe Shabbat. ________
2. ride to services. ________
3. help the poor. ________
4. have a Christmas tree on Hanukkah. ________
5. light candles on Friday evening. ________
6. work for the release of Soviet Jews. ________
7. eat bread at the seder. ________
8. give women an aliyah to the Torah. ________
9. support the State of Israel. ________
10. use an organ at Shabbat services. ________
11. fast on Yom Kippur. ________
12. decide for yourself how to be a good Jew. ________

Chapter Five lists many other things that make all Jews part of the same people. How many of them can you find? Here is one to start you off:

All Jews follow the same religious calendar.

____

____

____

____

____

____

____

MOVEMENTS

We don't like to speak of Orthodox, Conservative or Reform as "denominations" in Judaism. Since we are all one religion, with different aspects, we prefer to speak of "movements." This chapter talks about the major movements in Judaism, and mentions some of the different components of each. Summarize below what you know about

ORTHODOX JUDAISM ______________________________

____

CONSERVATIVE JUDAISM ______________________________

____

REFORM JUDAISM ______________________________

____

*FINDING MEANING**

All of the following words appear in Part One of the text. Here is your chance to be certain you know what they mean. Write the correct word next to its definition. (Watch out—there are some extra words that aren't defined!)

ALIYAH EMANCIPATION EXOTIC GOOD DEEDS FOOL HAFTARAH HASIDISM KIPPAH MIKVEH MIDRASH MIGRATION MITZVAH PATRILINEAL PIYYUTIM RECONSTRUCTIONISM TEFILLAH TZEDAKAH YESHIVAH YIDDISH

---

1. ____________________ The legal establishment of the Jews as full citizens, with privileges and responsibilities equal to those of all other citizens.

2. ____________________ A language constructed mostly of German and Hebrew, with some Russian and Slavic words, written in Hebrew characters. It was the native language of most Jews in Central and Eastern Europe.

3. ____________________ A divine commandment. The term has also come to mean "good deed."

4. ____________________ Liturgical poems, composed from around the 5th century until the 18th century. They were generally incorporated into the worship services to supplement existing prayers.

5. ____________________ The term is used for two specific kinds of "going up." It refers to people who move to Israel (those who go on ______). In the synagogue, one who has an ______ is "called up" to chant the blessings that precede and follow the Torah portion.

6. ____________________ An institution devoted to the study of Jewish learning.

7. ____________________ The skullcap (yarmulke) worn by all traditional and many Reform Jews during religious services and at meals. Today some women, particularly in liberal congregations, also choose to wear one during worship.

8. ____________________ Literally, righteousness or justice. The "righteous acts" that include charity to the needy and disadvantaged.

9. ____________________ "The prayer," also known as *amidah* (the "standing" prayer), is the central prayer of every Jewish worship service, for which all worshipers traditionally stand.

10. ____________________ A religious movement in Judaism, begun in Eastern Europe in the eighteenth century by the Baal Shem Tov, or Master of the Good Name. It encouraged Jews to draw close to God by singing, dancing and spiritual excitement.

DIARY: COMMON MEMORY

Common historical memory is one thing that all Jews share. The Holocaust and the creation of the modern State of Israel are perhaps the two most important events in Jewish history in this century. What makes them part of this "common memory"? (Get help from Chapter Five.) Then think about some of the major historical events during your own lifetime. What are they, and will any of them become part of our common Jewish memory?

6: The Reform Jewish Emphasis on Personal Freedom

GETTING THE PICTURE

Look at the photographs of different synagogues on page 52. Does your temple look like any of these?______ If it does, in what ways?____

____

If it doesn't, how is it different?____

____

____

____

In the space below, make a sketch of your synagogue. Or, if you prefer, attach a photograph that you have taken yourself.

WHAT DO YOU DO?

On page 55, the textbook tells us that freedom, which is so important to Reform Judaism, can be dangerous unless it is used wisely. Here are some things that involve making your own decisions and being responsible for yourself. What should you do in each situation? (What *do* you do?)

You parents give you lunch money (or allowance).
WHAT DO YOU DO WITH IT? (What *should* you do?)

____

____

____

You have a test tomorrow and your parents aren't home.
You really should study but your friends keep calling on the phone, and one of them has a problem she wants to talk about.
WHAT DO YOU DO? (What *should* you do?)

____

____

____

People you know have begun drinking beer and other alcoholic beverages. You know your parents don't want you to (and that it is illegal at your age), but you feel very tempted—and are embarrassed to be the only kid who says no.
WHAT DO YOU DO? (What *should* you do?)

____

____

____

Very soon you will be getting a driver's license.
HOW WILL YOU DRIVE? (How *should* you drive?)

____

____

____

DIARY:
BECAUSE WE ARE FREE

Write down five things you have done today that you were able to do because you are a Reform Jew living in a free country.

Examples:

I left my house without needing an identity card.
I (respectfully) disagreed with my teacher in religious school.

7 Changing Times and the Changes in Reform Judaism

FREEDOM IS A GIFT

Did you have to fight a long battle with your parents for the right to stay up late on Saturday night to watch television? Was it a thrilling victory to finally see the old bedtime go by with you still "legally" awake? You were free of a restriction that felt like a punishment. But what if you discovered that after the first few weeks the TV programs were boring or that you really got too tired to stay up that late? What did you do? Did you choose to go to bed earlier than you had to? Or did you force yourself to stay awake to make sure that no one challenged your right to stay up, or says, "I told you so"? If you stop and think about it, your decision probably depended on which type of freedom is most precious to you—"freedom from," "freedom to do" or "freedom not to do." In a way, of course, these aren't different freedoms but different ways of making the right choice.

Using this example (or another situation in which you were given a new freedom to make decisions), answer these questions.

What do you think is the right choice in such a situation? ______________________

Did you (or would you have) made the right decision? ______________________

____

RIGHT CHOICES

How do you make the right choices? Making choices is an important part of Reform Judaism—but it isn't always easy. Too often, people simply choose "not to do" because they are lazy, or because they think that since Reform Judaism gives them license to choose "freedom from" they will take the easy way out of obligations. That was never the intention of the people who shaped and guided our movement. Are there things you should have done but didn't because you were able to "get away with it"?

Write one here: ______________________________________

____

Outdoor Shabbat services at Eisner Camp.

CHANGES IN HISTORY

A number of very significant events are described in Chapter Seven. Write down one change that took place as a result of each of the following:

The Temple was destroyed by the Romans in 70 C.E.______________________________

____

The Emancipation allowed Jews to live in non-Jewish neighborhoods and work at jobs not restricted exclusively to Jews. ____

____

The Holocaust (1939–1945) murdered 6 million European Jews.__________________________

____

Israel became an independent country (1948).____________________________________

____

PICTURE THIS

On pages 62-64 are photographs of people at three different parades. Every parade is special. Decide what is special about each of these parades and write your answer here.

page 62: ______________________________

____

page 63: ______________________________

____

page 64: ______________________________

____

*SCRAMBLED IDEAS**

Here are five ideas about modern Reform Judaism. They've gotten jumbled and need to be set straight. All of these ideas appear, in almost the same (unscrambled) words, in the chapter.

1. observing use be People freedom Jews loyal their to should

   ____

2. first Jew good ethical mean a person Being to an ought all of being

   ____

3. same ideals Judaism are ethical The America values of the taught as by the

   ____

4. Jewish to live life fully a more freedom Reform use Jews their

   ____

5. caring Jews "Love just neighbor people not means for all for your as yourself"

   ____

OBLIGATIONS

We would like you to make a list of different kinds of Jewish obligations (your teacher can help you with ideas), and then put them into categories—"I already do" and "I choose not to do."

Here are some examples you may use if you wish:
- Lighting candles on Shabbat.
- Skipping religious school.
- Visiting a friend whose parent has died.
- Volunteering to help clean up a local Jewish cemetery.
- Going to services on a Jewish holiday.
- Keeping kosher.

I Already Do	**I Choose Not to Do**
______________________________	______________________________
______________________________	______________________________
______________________________	______________________________
______________________________	______________________________
______________________________	______________________________
______________________________	______________________________
______________________________	______________________________
______________________________	______________________________
______________________________	______________________________
______________________________	______________________________

Think about why you do—or do not do—what you have written. Would you describe yourself as *satisfied*, *dissatisfied*, or *not certain yet* about the kind of Jewish life you have chosen? ____________________

DIARY:
MY FAMILY AND ISRAEL

Think about the importance of Israel to you and your family. In what ways has Israel made a difference to your family—and your family to Israel? Write some of them below. (Possibilities include contributing to the United Jewish Appeal, purchasing of Israel Bonds and trees for the Jewish National Fund, visits to Israel, pen pals, relatives who live in Israel, Israel's position in the world, concern about specific issues in the news and many other ideas we haven't mentioned. Write these if they apply to you; if not, write what *does*.)

A temple youth group, touring Israel, visits a Jewish National Fund forest to plant tree saplings.

8: The Limits of Reform Jewish Freedom

WHO ARE YOU ANYWAY?

Reread the story about Reb Zusya (on pages 70-71 of the text). What is Reb Zusya really concerned about? ______________________________

____

How do you know if you are living up to your own potential? ______________________________

____

____

*ONE OR THE OTHER**

Write T or F next to each sentence.

1. There are no limits to a Reform Jew's freedom. ________
2. The CCAR approves of rabbis co-officiating with a priest or minister so long as the wedding ceremony takes place in a synagogue. ________
3. Being Jewish is not something you are all by yourself. ________
4. If there had been a strong State of Israel in the early 1940s, Jewish refugees from Nazi Europe would have found safety and freedom there. ________
5. The Reform movement and the Hasidic movement are remarkably similar in matters of personal style, religious mood and practice, but *not* in belief. ________
6. There is no such thing as a religious Reform Jew. ________

PRAYING

What are the things you think about when you pray to God? ______________________

____

____

Why? ______________________

____

ON KASHRUT

Most Reform Jews don't keep kosher. They may feel that eating habits are not an effective way of expressing their religiosity, or that, kashrut intentionally separates people from their neighbors. But some Reform Jews choose not to eat shellfish or pork products. They may create a liberal kind of kashrut because they want a modern way to carry on an old, precious Jewish tradition. Other Reform Jews may observe traditional kashrut in their homes because they want their parents and observant members of the Jewish community to be able to eat at their table. A small minority keeps kosher all the time because they feel that it is an important way of expressing their belief and identifying with the Jewish people. All these opinions and practices—as well as many others—are found in the Reform Jewish community.

How would you describe your family's way of keeping/not keeping kosher? ______________________

____

What will you do when you have your own kitchen? ______________________

____

Does knowing what other people choose to do help in making this decision? ______________________

What will happen if you want to marry someone whose way of observing Judaism is different from yours? ______________________

____

Is what a person eats an important or unimportant part of that person's Jewish identity? ______________________

Why? ______________________

____

____

FINDING THE WORDS FOR IT

ANTI-SEMITISM BELIEF CARING COMMUNITY FAITH FREEDOM GOD GOODNESS HASIDISM INTERMARRIAGE ISRAEL JUDAISM KNOWLEDGE LIMITS OBLIGATION PARADOX REFORM SELF-RESPECT SHABBAT TEN COMMANDMENTS TORAH TRADITION

T	R	A	D	I	T	I	O	N	I	S	R	A	E	L
E	F	G	M	R	O	F	E	R	N	A	C	D	G	H
N	Q	P	N	O	S	E	G	I	T	O	R	A	H	A
C	O	M	M	U	N	I	T	Y	E	Q	K	L	B	N
O	B	S	T	V	W	L	X	A	R	R	Z	P	X	T
M	L	M	S	E	V	E	N	H	M	X	I	Q	U	I
M	I	I	F	E	W	B	A	T	A	B	B	A	H	S
A	G	R	M	Q	N	P	B	I	R	C	X	Z	A	E
N	A	O	M	I	T	D	C	A	R	I	N	G	S	M
D	T	J	O	P	T	X	O	F	I	Q	L	M	I	I
M	I	Y	D	I	Y	S	F	O	A	B	N	S	D	T
E	O	O	E	E	O	O	E	I	G	O	D	I	I	I
N	N	N	E	E	A	E	I	O	E	U	Y	A	S	S
T	X	F	R	P	A	R	A	D	O	X	Q	D	M	M
S	E	L	F	R	E	S	P	E	C	T	W	U	H	O
Z	X	E	G	D	E	L	W	O	N	K	Y	J	V	U

BELIEF IN TORAH*

Read about Reform Judaism's belief in Torah (in Chapter Eight) and summarize it here. ______________

____

____

Do you agree with this position? ______________ Why or why not? ______________

____

____

DIARY: THINKING ABOUT GOD

Many people say that they don't think much about God—or even that they don't believe in God. And yet there are moments—when we are hurt or afraid, when someone we love is very ill, when something especially wonderful has happened, when we are eager for things to go a particular way—in which we pray to the God we aren't sure we believe in, or express our gratitude. How would you describe your own "relationship" with God?

9: Organizations of Reform Judaism

LOGOS

An organization's logo (the sign it chooses to use as an identifying picture), says a lot about the organization and how it sees itself. Look at the logos on page 80 of your textbook. Choose one and sketch it below.

What letters/words/sayings are on it? In what language(s)? What does the logo make you think about the organization?

____

____

____

WANTING IN

Read about the organizations that are described in Chapter Nine. Your assignment is to investigate a Reform Jewish organization and learn about its activities. Choose the one that you like best.

Which will you select? ______________________________

What are your reasons? ______________________________

____

GETTING THE PICTURE

Pages 76 and 77 show pairs of similar but different pictures. Describe the contrasts between these photographs.

____

____

BEING A RABBI

The Hebrew Union College-Jewish Institute of Religion trains rabbis to serve the Reform movement. What does a Reform rabbi need to be trained to do? Write a job description for a rabbi. In addition to the information in Chapter Nine, think about what your own rabbi does.

____

____

____

____

Leading a group singing session at Camp Eisner. These song-leaders are getting a good training in leadership. What kinds of qualities are required to be a good leader?

THE UNION

People have gotten accustomed to calling the UAHC "the Union," but sometimes they seem to forget what the term actually means. A congregation that is part of the Union of American Hebrew Congregations cannot exercise total freedom. Yet congregations join because there is strength in that Union. List some advantages and disadvantages of being part of the UAHC.

Advantages

Example:
Helping the congregation find the right rabbi.

Disadvantages

Example:
Having to pay dues to the Union.

*FINDING MEANING**

All of the following words and names appear in Part Two of *Explaining Reform Judaism.* Write the correct word next to its definition. (Not every word has a matching definition.)

ANTI-SEMITISM BAECK CHAUTAUQUA COMMUNION HOLOCAUST
INTERMARRIAGE YAHEL MAHZOR MEZUZAH OCONOMOWOC
PARADOX RABBI REVELATION SAGES

---

1. ________________ ("my teacher") An ordained scholar and teacher.

2. ________________ Hostility to and discrimination against Jews as a people.

3. ________________ "Cyclical" The festival prayer book, so called because the book follows the cycle of the Jewish festival calendar. Today we mostly use the word for the High Holy Days prayer book.

4. ________________ The first kibbutz in Israel founded by the Reform movement.

5. ________________ A parchment scroll containing the first two verses of the Shema, placed in a small decorative case and affixed to the right doorpost of every Jewish home, as commanded in the Torah ("you shall write them on the doorposts of your house . . ."). It is a visible reminder of God's presence.

6. ________________ Nazi Germany's attempt to destroy the entire Jewish population of Europe during World War II (1939-1945). Six million Jews were murdered, among them over 1 million children.

7. ________________ The marriage between two people of different religions; specifically, between a Jew and a non-Jew.

8. ________________ The teachers and scholars of the Jewish people during the period of the Talmud.

10: About God

BELIEF

It isn't easy to talk about God—what God is like, what we do or do not believe, and how we express what we know and believe. For that reason, we have included many different exercises to help you with this difficult chapter. Start by summarizing your own beliefs. Complete the following sentences.

I believe (or don't believe) in God because ______________________________

____

I see God in______________________________

I find God in my synagogue ______________________________

and when______________________________

When I am alone, I think of God as ______________________________

My favorite verse about God in *Gates of Prayer* is ______________________________

____

I would like to be able to communicate to God by______________________________

____

GOD TALK

These two passages from *Gates of Prayer* appear on page 86 of the textbook:
"Days pass and the years vanish, and we walk sightless among miracles."

"Were the sun to rise but once a year, we would all cry out: How great are Your works O God, and how glorious! Our hymns would rise up, our thanks would ascend. O God, Your wonders are endless, yet we do not see!"

What are these passages saying about God?______________________________

____

What are they saying about human beings? ______________________________

____

Do you agree?______________________________

EVIL

Bad things happen in everyone's life. This is something bad that has happened in my life: ________

____

____

____

When I had that experience, I (place a check next to whatever applies)

______Talked to my friends.

______Consulted my parents.

______Spoke to my teacher(s).

______Met with the rabbi.

______Talked with a doctor.

______Worked out my problem by myself.

______Discovered that human help was impossible.

______Called on God.

______Did not think about God.

What do you think helped most, and what would you do next time you confront a difficult or troubling problem? ____

____

____

EXPRESSING YOURSELF

"I believe in the sun even when it is not shining. I believe in love even when I do not feel it. I believe in God even when He is silent." (See page 88 of the text.) Have you thought about the meaning of this quotation? Do you agree with it? Write your thoughts here.

____

____

____

PARTNERS

Do you ever feel that you are God's "partner"? We have suggested some of the times that people feel they are in "partnership" with God. Check the ones that you think apply to you—and write some of your own.

______Helping my mom or dad with my little brother or sister.

______Taking care of my pet.

______Planting flowers in the garden.

______Taking out the garbage.

______Giving coins to someone who is begging on the street.

______Visiting the old man who lives near my house.

______Writing letters to my Senators and the President about political and social issues.

______Attending worship services at my temple.

______Going for a walk.

______Working at a car wash to raise money for *tzedakah*.

______Throwing my gum wrappers into a trash can instead of littering the street.

____

____

____

____

TRYING TO PRAY

The words in a prayer are sometimes hard to understand—especially if you are trying to communicate to a God who has power but whom we cannot "see." See if this idea works for you. "I want to communicate with God, but I don't know how. I don't even know how to say what I want to say. I know that God has no 'ears' that can hear words. Sometimes I use the words of my ancestors because the act of praying can give me comfort." Use your own words to express the same idea.

____

____

____

*JUSTICE FOR ALL**

From the earliest days of our people's history, we have been bothered by the problem of evil. It is bad enough that humans are imperfect—but what about God? The textbook quotes Abraham, Moses and Rabbi Levi Yitzhak of Berditchev. Make these sentences read correctly, and think about the passionate intensity they express. Then write the idea behind each statement in your own words.

Torah own laws the actions Judge of Your according to.

____

____

justly Judge not all of the Should deal the earth?

____

____

people O You upon harm why this Lord, did bring?

____

____

A Mitzvah Corps volunteer and children at an inner-city playground in New Brunswick, New Jersey.

AFTER LIFE

Within Judaism, as the textbook tells you, there are different beliefs about life after death. Reread page 89 to help you answer these questions:

What did some Jews believe would happen at the "end of days"? ______________________________

____

What are the two components of a human being? ______________________________

Spirit is another name for ______________________________

How did some early Reform Jews think people become immortal? ______________________________

____

Why is a system of ultimate reward and punishment important to many people? ______________

____

What is another way of saying "ultimate reward and punishment"? ______________________

____

LIFE AND DEATH

Do you ever wonder about what happens after a person dies? The pattern of life—the seasons that come and go in proper order, the fact that cuts and bruises heal, that babies are born and people grow up—is a kind of reminder that God lives forever. What is your reaction to this statement?

____

____

____

Has someone close to you ever died? What did you think about death then?

____

What did you think about God then?

____

Have your thoughts changed between then and now?

____

THE THIRTEEN ATTRIBUTES

One of the most famous passages in Jewish liturgy comes from the Torah (Exodus 34:6-7). In it, God tells Moses about God's own self. It has become known as the Thirteen Attributes of God.

> ***"The Lord! The Lord! A God compassionate and gracious, slow to anger, rich in steadfast kindness and truth, extending kindness to the thousandth generation, forgiving iniquity, transgression, and sin."***

Here are the thirteen attributes (qualities) of God, as derived from this passage by the great Jewish philosopher Maimonides:

1. Merciful before human actions
2. Merciful after human actions
3. Almighty
4. Compassionate
5. Gracious
6. Slow to anger
7. Abounding in kindness
8. Truthful
9. Remembering human merit
10. Forgiving iniquity
11. Forgiving transgression
12. Forgiving sin
13. Unlimited mercy

What do these attributes really mean? Use the first line after each number to define each of them in your own words.

1. ____
____

2. ____
____

3. ____
____

4. ____
____

5. ____
____

6. ______________________________

____

7. ______________________________

____

8. ______________________________

____

9. ______________________________

____

10. ______________________________

____

11. ______________________________

____

12. ______________________________

____

13. ______________________________

____

By trying to adopt God's attributes we make ourselves better people, only "a little lower than the angels." Now go back to your list, and in the second line after each attribute, write something that you do (or can do) to exhibit that quality and make yourself the best person you are capable of becoming.

DIARY: DAY BY DAY

Think back over the past week. As well as you can remember them, record here your experiences that "prove" God's existence. (Hints: think about nature, sickness and health, love, kindness, etc.)

Sunday

Monday

Tuesday

Wednesday

Thursday

Friday

Shabbat

11: About the Jewish People

GETTING THE PICTURE

The photograph on page 95 shows a Baltimore Reform congregation's tangible commitment to the Zionist cause. How can you tell? ______________________________

____

THE JEWISH PEOPLE

There is something special about being part of the Jewish people. It can make us feel as if we have relatives all over the world. What are some of the ways you feel this connection? We'll start you off with two suggestions:

Kissing people on Friday night after services.

Singing *Hatikvah,* the Israeli national anthem.

Now add your own:

____

____

____

____

____

When you meet someone for the first time, do you feel closer to that person when you learn he or she is Jewish? Why or why not? ______________________________

What do you expect to have in common with the person?______________________________

____

WHEN YOU STOP AND THINK ABOUT IT

How many of your closest friends are Jewish? ______________________

Does that make a difference in your life?________Why or why not? ______________________

____

____

EATING

Complete these sentences: I feel that I am eating "Jewish food" when I eat____________. It gives me a special feeling of belonging to a people. My favorite Jewish food is____________.

It originally comes from____________.

Now list some other foods that are thought of as Jewish.

____

____

____

____

____

DEFINITIONS

Judaism can be defined as a religion, a nation, a people or as all three. Write the definition of each below.

Judaism is a religion because ______________________

Judaism is a nation because ______________________

Judaism is a people because ______________________

Does any one of these satisfy your idea of Judaism? If yes, which one and why?____________

____

If not, write your own definition of Judaism.______________________

____

CHOOSING JUDAISM

After you have looked at the ways the textbook says people can become Jewish, answer the following:

If I were not born Jewish, I would choose to become a Jew by ______________________________

____

Go back to page 19 of this workbook (in Chapter Four) and see how your answer now compares to what you wrote there. Have you changed your mind? If yes, why? ______________________________

____

SCRAMBLED WORDS*

Here is a list of some Jewish languages, foods, customs, and holidays. The words have been scrambled. Unscramble each word, using the correct spellings provided in the box. Then decide which of the three aspects of Judaism—religious, national, or ethnic—the term represents. Classify each term by writing an R (religious aspect), N (national aspect), or E (ethnic aspect) next to it. (Some of the terms may fit into more than one category.)

MATZAH TU B'SHEVAT YIDDISH ROSH HASHANAH JUDEO-ARABIC KUGEL SEDER SUKKAH ARAMAIC FELAFEL

1. SIDYIHD ____________________
2. CARAIMA ____________________
3. UT H'BEVATS ____________________
4. GLUEK ____________________
5. UKHASK ____________________
6. AZMATH ____________________
7. SHOR ANSHAHAH ____________________
8. DEUJO-BRAICA ____________________
9. FLEAFLE ____________________
10. DRESE ____________________

Compare answers with your classmates. Are you surprised at how many terms fit into more than one category? Or at how difficult it is even to classify them? Is Judaism easily divided into separate categories? Why or why not?

____

____

____

ZIONISM FOR AMERICAN JEWS

What "nation" problems were the early Reformers in America worried about? ______________________

____

What things did they do to be sure no one could accuse them of supporting Zionism? ______________

____

____

What made Reform Jews in America become strong supporters of Israel? __________________________

____

____

Do you ever feel a sense of conflict between your loyalty to America and your loyalty to Israel?

When? ____

____

Express your hopes (prayer) for Israel ____

____

Express your hopes (prayer) for America ____

____

Youth group members enjoying a Purim party at their synagogue.

DIARY: MY FAMILY'S OBSERVANCE

List some of the things that you and your family do in observance of Reform Judaism.

Examples:

We belong to a synagogue.
We light candles on Friday night.
We attend services on Shabbat and holidays.

Now list some of the things that other families do that you might want to include in your own family's observance.

12: About the Torah, the Bible and Jewish Tradition

TORAH

Do you believe that Moses received the Torah from God and wrote down all the words? If not, what is your explanation?________________________________

____

____

Listening, discussing, and learning at a camp Torah seminar.

SHABBAT*

Here are the verses about Shabbat that appear in the two versions of the Ten Commandments. Compare the two passages and then answer the questions that follow them.

Exodus 20:8-11:

"Remember the Sabbath day and keep it holy. Six days you shall labor and do all your work, but the seventh day is a Sabbath of the Lord your God: you shall not do any work—you, your son or daughter, your male or female slave, or your cattle, or the stranger who is within your settlements. For in six days the Lord made heaven and earth and sea, and all that is in them, and He rested on the seventh day; therefore the Lord blessed the Sabbath day and hallowed it."

Deuteronomy 5:12-15:

"Observe the Sabbath day and keep it holy, as the Lord your God has commanded you. Six days you shall labor and do all your work, but the seventh day is a Sabbath of the Lord your God: you shall not do any work—you, your son or your daughter, your male or female slave, your ox or your ass, or any of your cattle, or the stranger in your settlements, so that your male and female slave may rest as you do. Remember that you were a slave in the land of Egypt and the Lord your God freed you from there with a mighty hand and an outstretched arm; therefore the Lord your God has commanded you to observe the Sabbath day."

1. Each passage begins with almost identical wording—except for one important difference. What is that difference?

   ____

2. How would you explain the difference in meaning of the two sentences?

   ____

3. In the second passage, it is written that we are commanded by God to observe Shabbat. Is the first selection a commandment as well, even though the word commandment is not mentioned?

   ____

4. Why do we rest according to Exodus 20:8-11? According to Deuteronomy 5:12-15? Do you prefer one reason to the other? Why?

   ____

   ____

   ____

MAN AND WOMAN

Here is another comparison. Both of these quotations from the beginning of the Torah describe the creation of human beings. Read each carefully and answer the questions that follow.

Genesis 1:26

"I will make man in My image, after My likeness. They shall rule the fish of the sea, the birds of the sky, the cattle, the whole earth, and all the creeping things that creep on earth."

Genesis 2:18-22

"The Lord God said, 'It is not good for man to be alone; I will make a fitting helper for him.' And the Lord God fashioned into a woman the rib that He had taken from the man, and He brought her to the man."

1. Do both passages mention the word "woman"? ____________________

2. Does the word "man," in the first passage, refer to only men, or to women as well?

   ____

3. In the first passage, the Bible changes from singular (man) in the first sentence to plural (they) in the second sentence. Why? (Hint: Look at your answer to the previous question.)

   ____

   ____

4. What is the function of man in the first passage as compared to function of woman in the second?

   ____

   ____

TRUE OR FALSE*

1. Reform Jews believe that "religious geniuses" talk to God all the time. ________
2. All human beings are God's "children." ________
3. Our ancestors were among the few ancient peoples that believed in one God. ________
4. Reform Jews believe that the Bible is the greatest of books. ________
5. We carry on the tradition of Torah when we make Judaism important in our lives. ________
6. The new discoveries of science make it hard for any thoughtful person to believe in God. ________

AN IMPERFECT CREATION

Why is the Bible in the *Guinness Book of World Records?* ________________________________

____

Reread the section titled "An Imperfect Creation," on pages 103-105 of the textbook. Were you surprised to learn that there may be inconsistencies in the Bible? What is the example given by the textbook? ____

How do you think this inconsistency occurred? ______________________________________

Can you offer any other examples? ____

For Shabbat services, campers change from their shorts and t-shirts to more formal clothing. How does putting on our best clothes contribute to the specialness of Shabbat?

DIARY: SHABBAT

Describe how you spent your most recent Shabbat. Was it typical? If not, then describe what you usually do on Shabbat. Then answer these questions:

Is there any way in which you make Shabbat special in your life?

What could you do to give your observance of Shabbat more meaning?

13: The Reform Jewish Emphasis on Ethics

*AMOS**

The prophet Amos took on a very difficult assignment. He had to convince the people of Israel to change the way they acted. After you have read about him in Chapter Thirteen, answer these questions.

1. In what century did Amos prophesy? ______
2. What was the name of the king of Israel at that time? ______
3. Where did Amos come from? ______
4. Where did Amos preach? ______
5. What did he say about Judah? ______
6. What did he say about Israel? ______
7. Why do you think Amos first criticized the enemies of Israel and then criticized Judah, leaving his criticism of Israel for last? ______

   ______

PERSONAL ETHICS

Reform Judaism chose prophetic Judaism as the model for its movement. The early Reformers emphasized the ethical aspects of Judaism because they were anxious to make their Judaism acceptable to the society that had just welcomed them. Moral commitment and ethical involvement have remained very important to Reform Judaism. How do ethics matter in your life (in sports, student government, exams, dealing with friends, etc.)? Please give several examples.

______

______

______

______

TRUE OR FALSE*

1. Amos allowed the people to make excuses for their actions. ________
2. Amos called the people of Israel hypocrites. ________
3. Amos was a prince in Egypt. ________
4. Amos was proud of all the sacrifices brought to the Temple. ________
5. Amos was friendly with Amaziah, a priest in Bethel. ________

HARD QUESTIONS

This exercise may be painful to do, but we think you'll feel better about yourself when you're finished. Complete the following:

I have sometimes been with friends who did unethical things (lying, stealing, etc.). This is what happened. ____

____

____

This is what I did. ____

____

This is something that I have done, even though I knew it was wrong to do. ________________

____

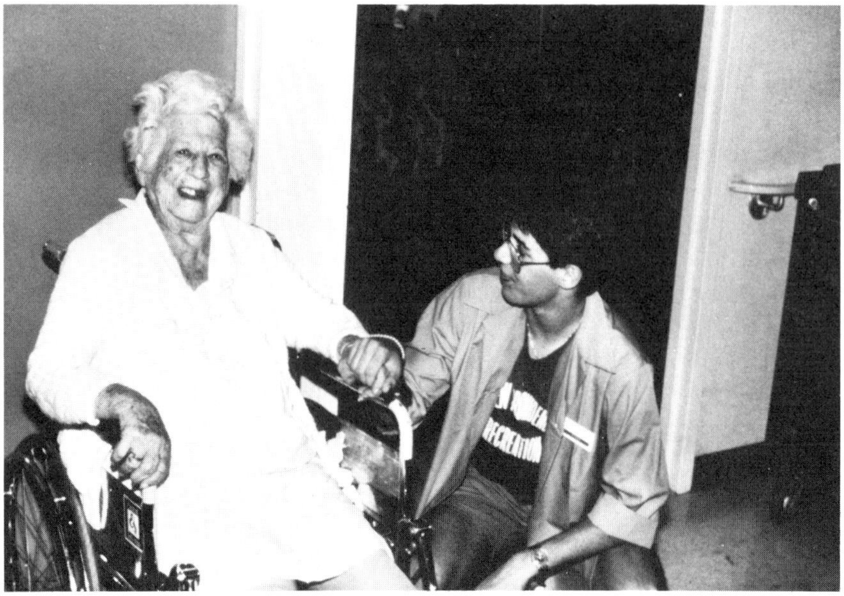

A resident of a nursing home and a Mitzvah Corps volunteer. What does this picture say about the ethical standards of Reform Judaism?

DIARY: WHY JUDAISM?

Read page 118 in the textbook and answer the following questions: If proper ethical behavior is the thrust of Reform Judaism, why do we need Judaism? Isn't good behavior enough? Why can't we just be ethical human beings and forget about being Jewish? Why should we want to remain Jewish?

Don't forget that this is a diary. Answer the questions from your own perspective, using the word "I" and drawing on your own experiences.

14: Reform Jewish Duties: Ethics Plus

REMINDERS

Wearing a kippah all the time is one of the ways a traditional Jewish man expresses his religious position and reminds himself of his Jewish obligations. How might you, as a liberal Jew, show who you are and remind yourself of your Jewish obligations?

Write your suggestions here. (Example: not eating dairy and meat products together.)

____

____

____

WHY THEY'RE WRONG

Judaism cannot be measured on a number line, with Reform at one end and Orthodoxy at the other. If you heard other people say that Reform Jews aren't religious (or that we *can't be* religious because we're Reform Jews), how would you feel?

____

How would you answer them? ____

____

MATURING

Do you think that, as you grow older, you may choose to do things differently from the way you do them now? Why? ____

____

DIARY: WEEK BY WEEK

Look at the nine categories of Reform obligation (on pages 120-123 in the textbook). Figure out specific ways that you can fulfill each of the obligations. (See page 124 for ideas.) Write your plans for carrying out these obligations throughout the rest of the school year.

ethical obligations

home and family

study

private prayer and public worship

daily religious observance

Shabbat and holidays

celebrating life-cycle events

involvement with synagogue and community

helping the Jewish people

15: How We Decide Just What We Need to Do

INTRODUCING CHANGE

When organized groups like congregations make major changes, the changes don't happen all by themselves. Many people take part in the decision-making; for example, when a congregation chooses to do something like change prayerbooks. Pretend you are a member of the ritual committee at your temple. The committee decides to replace the old Reform prayerbook with the new one, *Gates of Prayer.* What would you say to convince the congregation? (Remember: people are used to the old book and buying the new one costs money.

____

____

____

____

UNEXPECTED RESULTS

Sometimes actions have consequences that weren't imagined (or foreseen) by the people who took them. For example, when citizenship rights were extended to everyone after the French Revolution, most of the very people who were anxious to grant these rights had forgotten that "everyone" would include Jews. So, too, with rights for women in Judaism. The photographs on page 132 show two examples of women's role in Jewish life. What are they?

____

Now list some specific things that the equality of men and women in liberal Judaism makes it possible for women to do:

____

____

____

____

____

THREE CASES

CASE I: WOMEN

Read Case One on pages 131-133 of the textbook. Write here how you feel about the equality of women in Judaism and in your synagogue.

CASE II: SUNDAY SABBATH

Now read Case Two (Pages 133-135). What is your reaction to the Reform movement's experiment of creating a Sunday Sabbath—and to its failure? Why do you think it failed?

CASE III: INTERMARRIAGE

Case Three (pages 136-139) deals with a subject that is still controversial. What is your opinion about rabbis performing mixed marriages? Would you feel the same way if someone (or no one) in your family was involved in a mixed marriage?

FREEDOM OF CHOICE FOR EVERYONE

Write here what you believe about people (including rabbis) being free to choose to do something that other people (including other rabbis) disagree with.

If you think that there are certain things no one should be free to do, does that make you a "bad" Reform Jew? Why or why not?

*CRASBELMD DROWS**

Unscramble the words below. Then unscramble the circled letters to create the mystery word. It is really what the entire chapter is about.

1. TRAINERGAIRME

   _ _ _ (_) _ _ _ _ _ _ _ _ _

   1. Marriage between two people from different backgrounds.

2. NOVERNIOCS

   (_) _ _ _ _ _ _ _ _ _

   2. The process a person undergoes to become Jewish.

3. TREPMEXINE

   _ _ _ _ _ (_) _ _ _ _

   3. A test to see if something does or doesn't work.

4. DYUNAS

   (_) _ _ _ _ _

   4. A day in the week.

5. INDROTANIO

   _ _ _ _ _ _ _ _ (_) _

   5. "Women cannot justly be denied the privilege of ____________."

6. NIMNAY

   _ _ (_) _ _ _

   6. The minimum number of Jews required for most prayers.

7. NIEBLINA

   _ _ _ _ _ (_) _ _

   7. "UAHC ____________ resolutions have supported women's rights."

8. STEXIS

   _ _ _ _ (_) _

   8. "We still have a lot to learn about how we can write prayers or refer to God in non- ____________ ways."

9. MERFODE

   _ _ _ _ (_) _ _

   9. Liberty.

The mystery word is ___ ___ ___ ___ ___ ___ ___ ___ ___

DIARY:
SOMETHING TO SING ABOUT

We usually take freedom for granted, but once in a while something reminds us of how lucky we are. When that happens, our pleasure at the feeling of freedom is so great that we want to shout or cry with joy, or laugh, or sing. Have you ever had that experience? Try writing a poem or song about freedom, or quote the lyrics of a song that talks about freedom.

16: Our Relation to the State of Israel

BEYOND DREAMS

"If you will it," Theodor Herzl wrote, "it is no dream." What did he mean?

IS AMERICA OUR JERUSALEM?

In the early days of Reform Judaism, there were many people who believed in the potential of America so much that they rejected the need for a Jewish state. That stage in the history of Reform Judaism is part of our legacy as Reform Jews. When you read about it, or someone says something to you about it, how do you react?

And what do you answer?

MESSAGE TO ISRAEL

A secular Israeli tells you he knows nothing about Reform Judaism. What should you tell him? What can Reform Judaism offer to Israelis?

SEE AND SAY

Look at the photographs in this chapter and read their captions. Then write a short essay about the kind of country you think Israel is. Make sure to mention every one of the photographs as supporting evidence.

____

____

____

____

____

ISRAEL TODAY

Israel has accomplished many great things, given the relatively few years of the state's existence and the difficult problems Israelis have had to face (not only hostile neighbors but absorbing many people from a wide variety of countries and cultural backgrounds). Here are six categories. Describe one achievement Israel has made in each of these areas. (Consult the textbook if you need help).

Education: ____

____

Medicine: ____

____

Technology: ____

____

Culture: ____

____

Environmental control: ____

____

Government: ____

____

OUR DUTIES TO ISRAEL

List five different ways American Jews should express their relationship to Israel:

____

____

____

____

____

WHICH IS WHICH*

Each of these definitions matches one of words that follow. Which goes with which? All of them have something to do with the Reform movement's involvement in Israel.

TEL DAN HAR CHALUTZ YAHEL AMERICAN COUNCIL FOR JUDAISM ARZA WUPJ

1. ____________________The organization that serves the Reform movement around the world; its headquarters are in Jerusalem.

2. ____________________The first Reform *mitzpeh* (settlement) in the northern part of Israel.

3. ____________________Teams from NFTY, HUC-JIR and other Reform groups have helped with the archeological excavations at places like this dig site.

4. ____________________The first kibbutz established by the Reform movement in Israel. It is the first non-Orthodox religious kibbutz.

5. ____________________The Association of Reform Zionists of America, the only organization that contributes a Reform Jewish perspective to world Zionist affairs.

6. ____________________The splinter group that formed to protest the Reform movement's support for the State of Israel.

DIARY: SOME DAY I'LL GO TO ISRAEL . . .

Have you ever thought about going to Israel for a year of college or to spend some time living on one of the Reform settlements there (Kibbutz Yahel, perhaps, or Har Chalutz)? Does the idea appeal to you? How do you think your parents would react?

Write a plan for your trip.

Tired but exhilarated after a steep climb, NFTY (National Federation of Temple Youth) members pose on top of Masada, the mountain in Israel where Jewish soldiers once held out against the legions of Rome.

17: Our Relation to the Jewish Community

GRAPHICS

The textbook describes our relationship to the Jewish world as a series of "nesting bowls." How else might that be expressed? Draw a chart or a diagram to show your relationship to the synagogue and the Jewish community (local, national and world)—and the fact that the synagogue and the community are related to one another as well. Start by putting the word "me" in the center.

TRUE OR FALSE*

1. Reform Jews care only about the organizations of the Reform movement; what the rest of the Jewish community does is not Reform's problem. ________
2. It is not important to belong to a synagogue or be active in the Jewish community so long as you *feel* very strongly and positively that you are Jewish. ________
3. Family life is the core of the Jewish community. ________
4. The organizations of the Jewish community are usually constituents or beneficiaries (that is, they get most of their funding from) of the local Federation. ________
5. The best way to protect Jewish civil rights is to mind our own business and only speak out on Jewish issues. ________
6. Going to regional conclaves and national conventions widens the personal Jewish community of the people who participate. ________

ALLOCATING SPACE

Why does the local Jewish community newspaper spend so much of its space on dinners, marriages, births, deaths and people receiving honors? ______________________________

____

____

PHOTO STORIES

On pages 158-159 are three photographs. Each was taken by an American Jewish tourist. Look at the pictures and read the captions. Choose one photograph. Imagine that you are the photographer who took the picture.

Why did you take it? ______________________________

What is your reaction to the "story" of the photograph? ______________________________

What questions might you want to ask the person or persons in the picture? ______________________________

____

*INITIALS**

Every Jewish organization seems to use initials to identify itself. Many people find it very confusing. There are many such organization in this chapter of the textbook. Can you figure out which is which?

1. ADL______________________
2. AIPAC______________________
3. AJC______________________ and ______________________
4. CRC______________________
5. NJCRAC______________________
6. YM-YWHA______________________

Here are some more initials mentioned in previous chapters. Can you remember what they stand for?

7. CCAR______________________
8. HUC-JIR______________________
9. NFTY______________________
10. WUPJ______________________
11. ARZA______________________

DIARY: MY SYNAGOGUE FAMILY

On pages 152-153, the textbook talks about ways in which many synagogues are extended "families." How does your synagogue serve that role for you and your family? Describe an event, such as holiday services, a bar or bat mitzvah, party, bazaar, etc., that made you feel that your synagogue was one big family.

18: Reaching Out to Our Country and the World

"COMMANDMENTS" FOR DEMOCRACY

List some of the new "commandments" that come with living in a democracy.

OUR RIGHTS

No matter how hard people try to get along with one another, there are bound to be conflicts. It seems to be a very human trait to try to blame other people when we can't solve our own problems. Since Jews are a very small percentage of the population in America (under 3%), we are often overlooked when basic decisions are made. Does your secular school hold classes on Rosh Hashanah or Yom Kippur? What about school dances or sports activities?

These are not anti-Semitic acts, only thoughtless ones. But sometimes we face anti-Semitism—on the school bus, in team sports, from a teacher or a neighbor. Have you had such an experience? Describe one thing that is going on now in your own life or in the life of your community that you would like help in resolving (or, if it has been resolved, how it got settled).

PICTURE THIS

Imagine that you are Uriah Phillips Levy. Write a letter to a friend telling about the fact that you helped abolish flogging in the United States Navy. With the photograph on page 161 as guidance, explain why flogging is bad and why you see abolishing it as a good Jewish accomplishment.

A UNIVERSAL MESSAGE

Reform Judaism teaches that we have obligations to everyone. List some of the Jewish teachings that are universal ethics. ____________________

____

____

How will you make them part of your own life? ____________________

____

WHAT WOULD YOU DO?

No one has enough time or money to do everything they would like to accomplish. People must therefore make choices and set priorities. Sometimes it is important to be concerned only about Jews; sometimes it is important to concentrate on activities outside the Jewish community. Real life is filled with hard decisions. What would you do in each of the following cases?

Two candidates are running for office. One strongly supports Israel, but you disagree with his positions on most other issues. The other supports Israel less enthusiastically, but you agree with most of his other positions. Whom would you vote for? Why?

____

____

____

You have worked hard to break down discrimination at the local country club. At last the club lifts its restriction against Jewish members. But just before you send in your membership dues you hear that blacks are still not admitted. Would you join? Why or why not?

____

____

____

MISSION IMPOSSIBLE?

Chapter Eighteen speaks of early Reform Judaism's "mission" to act as a "light to the nations." Describe what was meant by a "light." Do you feel this mission to be valid today?

"A toast to the future!"

*FINDING MEANING**

All of these words appear in Parts Three, Four and Five of the text. Most of them, but not all, are defined below. Test your Jewish vocabulary by writing the correct word before its meaning.

ALEINU ARAMAIC CONVERT FEDERATION FLOGGING HAVDALAH HEVRA HUPPAH KASHRUT MESSIAH MILAH MUSAF MYSTICISM PARTICULARISM SHABBAT TRANSGRESSIONS

---

1. ____________________ Literally, a group of friends; by extension, a volunteer group or society.

2. ____________________ the dietary laws of traditional Judaism.

3. ____________________ ("It is incumbent upon us . . .") A concluding prayer, and one of the most important in the entire prayer book.

4. ____________________ An early Semitic language closely related to Hebrew and using the same alphabet. Much of the Talmud is in this language, as are a number of major prayers, including the Kol Nidre on Yom Kippur eve and the Kaddish.

5. ____________________ The Jewish Sabbath, from sundown on Friday to after dark on Saturday night.

6. ____________________ ("separation") The short religious ceremony marking the conclusion of Shabbat and its separation from the new week. Blessings are made over a cup of wine, a braided candle and a spice box.

7. ____________________ The canopy held over the heads of the bride and groom during a Jewish wedding ceremony.

8. ____________________ The "additional" service recited in traditional congregations in memory of the animal sacrifice at the Temple in Jerusalem. Reform Judaism took this out of the prayer-book.

9. ____________________ Someone not born to Jewish parents who chooses to become a Jew.

10. ____________________ The king or Savior appointed by God to rule over Israel and all the world at the "end of days," ushering in a time of peace and happiness for everyone. Reform Jews substituted for this word a belief in a time when all human beings would cease to do evil, and humankind would thereby be redeemed, creating the "kingdom of God."

11. ____________________ (known in Hebrew as *Kabbalah*) An attempt to know God and comprehend God's majesty. For Jewish mystics, every human act is filled with great spiritual significance and provides an opportunity to draw closer to God.

19: Our Hope for the Messianic Age

END OF DAYS

Compare the traditional view of a Messiah to the Reform idea of a Messianic Era.

Which makes more sense to you, and why?

FALSE PROOFS

What are some of the "proofs" fundamentalist Christians give to show that our Bible predicts the coming of Jesus?

What is wrong with each argument or example?

HARD TRUTHS

Reform Judaism is realistic about human nature. It understands that human beings may not live up to their potential. What, according to the chapter, are some of the bad things done by human beings in this century?

____

____

Now give some of the chapter's examples of goodness. ____________________

____

FIND THE HIDDEN WORDS

Can you find in this mix of letters eighteen words relevant to Reform Judaism and this book? They are hidden horizontally, vertically and diagonally.

REFORM MITZVAH LIBERAL CREATIVE GOD WISE
SCHOLARSHIP ENGLISH CHOICE TORAH ZOHAR WOMEN
EMANCIPATION TEMPLE EQUAL ETHICS PROPHETS
HEBREW CONFIRMATION

E	C	M	R	O	F	E	R	A	B	N	C
N	H	M	I	T	Z	V	A	H	X	O	O
G	O	D	Q	O	B	R	H	A	B	I	N
L	I	B	E	R	A	L	O	E	C	T	F
I	C	S	G	A	H	G	Z	F	D	A	I
S	E	I	R	H	E	B	R	E	W	P	R
H	C	R	E	A	T	I	V	E	O	I	M
E	J	L	M	R	E	S	A	R	M	C	A
K	Q	N	O	T	M	L	P	Q	E	N	T
V	C	U	H	A	P	T	R	S	N	A	I
X	B	I	A	Z	L	U	H	J	K	M	O
W	C	Y	D	L	E	G	W	I	S	E	N
S	C	H	O	L	A	R	S	H	I	P	T
M	N	S	T	E	H	P	O	R	P	L	U

WE THEREFORE HOPE

Write your own conclusion to the sentence. in the middle of page 176 of the textbook, from the final paragraph of the *Aleinu* (Adoration): "We therefore hope, O Lord, Our God, soon to behold . . .

___

___

___

PHOTO ALBUM

You began this book with some personal photographs. Now add some more that have been taken during the past year. How have you changed? How have you stayed the same?

Ask your teacher to designate a "photo day." Elect one classmate, or your teacher, to bring in a camera and take a picture of the entire class. If possible, the photographer should make enough copies to give one to everybody. Attach yours to this page, along with a caption that will make you smile when you see it, years from now.

DIARY: A COMMITMENT TO JUDAISM

We hope that completing this workbook has helped you understand about being a Reform Jew—and that you are proud to be one. If you were to share a few of the most important things you have found out about Reform Judaism with your friends, what would you tell them? Write your answers here and, just before your Confirmation, read this again and see, at the time when you are ready to confirm your commitment to an adult Jewish life, how well you understood Reform Judaism today.

(signature)

(date)

ANSWER KEY

page 6 IDENTIFIERS red cloth badges, yellow cloth badges, peculiar "Jews' hats."

page 8 SCRAMBLED WORDS 1. Jacobson 2. Seesen 3. Emanicipation 4. ghetto 5. Revolution 6. France 7. Germany; REFORM

page 9 THE FRENCH REVOLUTION 1. People's insistence on governing themselves. 2. The rights of citizenship (voting, ownership of property, education, etc.). 3. Set an example for the granting of citizenship rights to Jews in other countries.

page 9 WHICH DON'T BELONG? 1. law, dentistry 2. Christian schools 3. church services, Christians and Jews worshipping together.

page 10 MORE OR LESS 1. more 2. less 3. more 4. more. Other reforms: prayers in German, organ music, mixed choir, sermon.

page 12 TRUE OR FALSE 1. F 2. F 3. F 4. T 5. F 6. T 7. F 8. T

page 13 WHAT AND HOW He ordered that Jewish services must be held only in existing synagogues, and that only the traditional ritual could be used. New types of services, like those at the Beer Temple in Berlin, were now illegal, and Reformers could not introduce any other changes into the synagogue service.

page 13 PROVING HIS POINT collections of midrash, biblical ideas, help with their own lives, sermons.

page 13 UNSCRAMBLE THIS When Leopold Zunz wanted to learn about the historical development of sermons, he had to unscramble many pieces of confusing information.

page 15 WAVES OF IMMIGRATION seventeenth century, Spanish and Portuguese, 1840s, Western Europe, Germany, 1881, 1924, Eastern Europe.

page 15 IDEALS OF AN ERA 1. B 2. D 3. A 4. C

page 16 A FILL-IN ON MESSIANISM 1. graves, souls, purified, Jerusalem. 2. spark, conscience, souls, dies.

page 21 A SAMPLE TEST 2. Yom Kippur 3. Sukkot 4. Simhat Torah

page 24 BAR AND BAT MITZVAH a recognition of growing older, or "coming of age." (Another good answer: reading from the Torah.)

page 25 COMMON TO ALL 1. T 2. F 3. T 4. F 5. T 6. T 7. F 8. F 9. T 10. F 11. T 12. F

page 27 FINDING MEANING 1. Emancipation 2. Yiddish 3. mitzvah 4. piyyutim 5. aliyah 6. yeshivah 7. kippah 8. tzedakah 9. tefillah 10. Hasidism

page 34 SCRAMBLED IDEAS 1. People should use their freedom to be loyal, observing Jews. 2. Being a good Jew ought first of all to mean being an ethical person. 3. The ethical ideals of America are

ANSWER KEY

the same as the values taught by Judaism. 4. Reform Jews use their freedom to live a more fully Jewish life. 5. "Love your neighbor as yourself" means caring for all people, not just for Jews.

page 37 ONE OR THE OTHER 1. F 2. F 3. T 4. T 5. F 6. F

page 44 FINDING MEANING 1. rabbi 2. anti-Semitism 3. mahzor 4. Yahel 5. mezuzah 6. Holocaust 7. intermarriage 8. Sages

page 48 JUSTICE FOR ALL 1. Judge Your own actions according to the laws of Torah. 2. Should not the Judge of all the earth deal justly? 3. O Lord, why did You bring harm upon this people?

page 55 SCRAMBLED WORDS 1. Yiddish (N,E) 2. Aramaic (N) 3. Tu b'Shevat (R,N) 4. kugel (E) 5. sukkah (R,N) 6. matzah (R,N,E) 7. Rosh Hashanah (R) 8. Judeo-Arabic (N,E) 9. felafel (E) 10. seder (R,N,E)

page 59 SHABBAT 1. One sentence begins with the word "Remember," the other with "Observe."

page 60 TRUE OR FALSE 1. F 2. T 3. T 4. T 5. T 6. F

page 63 AMOS 1. 8th century B.C.E. 2. Jereboam 3. Judah 4. Bethel (in Israel) 5. The people there have ignored God and the laws of the Torah. 6. The people there were more concerned with wealth than with justice. 7. An effective tactic in making a persuasive speech. With each step he brought God's judgements closer to the people listening.

page 64 TRUE OR FALSE 1. F 2. T 3. F 4. F 5. F.

page 70 CRASBELMD DROWS 1. intermarriage 2. conversion 3. experiment 4. Sunday 5. ordination 6. minyan 7. Biennial 8. sexist 9. freedom; DECISIONS

page 74 WHICH IS WHICH 1. WUPJ (World Union for Progressive Judaism) 2. Har Chalutz 3. Tel Dan 4. Yahel 5. ARZA 6. American Council for Judaism

page 76 TRUE OR FALSE 1. F 2. F 3. T 4. T 5. F 6. T

page 77 INITIALS 1. Anti-Defamation League (of B'nai Brith) 2. American-Israel Public Affairs Committee 3. American Jewish Congress and American Jewish Committee 4. Community Relations Advisory Council 5. National Jewish Community Relations Council 6. Young Men's/Young Women's Hebrew Association 7. Central Conference of American Rabbis 8. Hebrew Union College-Jewish Institute of Religion 9. National Federation of Temple Youth 10. World Union for Progressive Judaism 11. Association of Reform Zionists of America

page 82 FINDING MEANING 1. hevra 2. kashrut 3. Aleinu 4. Aramaic 5. Shabbat 6. Havdalah 7. huppah 8. Musaf 9. convert 10. messiah 11. mysticism